Dedicated to:
Ben & Mary

Written by: Abigail Gartland

Hello, my name is St. Vincent De Paul!

I was born in France in 1581!

When I was a young man, I wanted to be a lawyer. As I grew older, I felt called to become a priest.

I was ordained into the priesthood in 1600. I was honored to dedicated my life to the church.

In France I stayed at a little church where I was able to help many poor people.

I loved taking care of people and teaching them about God.

I created an order of priests called the Vincentians to devote our lives to praying and helping people.

The Vincentians were called to serve the poor.

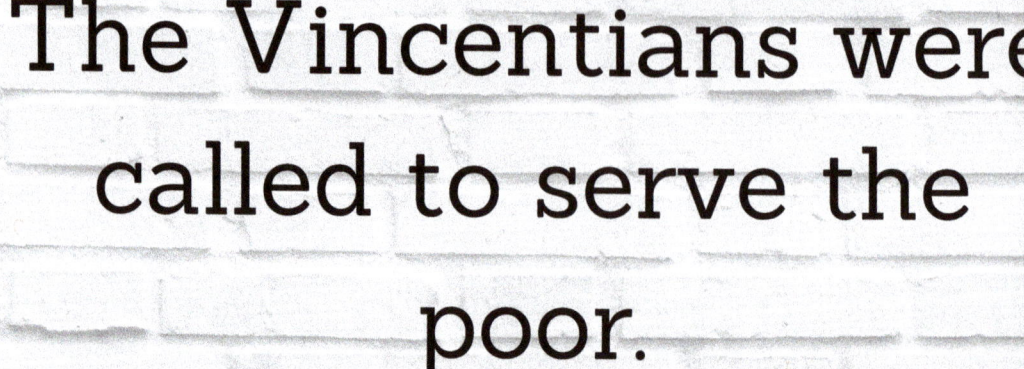

How can you help the poor?

You can help at a food kitchen to make sure everyone has a nice meal.

You can be kind to everyone, and remember that we are all God's children.

Do you want to be more like me?

You can celebrate my feast day with me on September 27th.

I am the patron saint of all works of charity.

Charity is when we love and serve others

I pray for you every day of your life.

St. Vincent De Paul, pray for us!

opyright:

part: © PentoolPixie © LimeandKiwiDesigns
ensed purchased: 1/10/2024

About the Author

Abigail Gartland

I love the saints and I love my faith. The idea for sharing the stories of the saints with little ones came when my dear friend were expecting their first baby. I wanted to create something as unique and special as our friendship. Each book is dedicated to very special people and groups who have enriched my faith in different ways. I am blessed to write these stories and appreciate the unending support of my family and friends. When I am not writing, am a middle school teacher. I hope you enjoy these stories. I pray for each and every person who opens one of my books to learn more about the saints.

Abbie

www.ingramcontent.com/pod-product-compliance
Lightning Source LLC
LaVergne TN
LVHW051044070526
838201LV00067B/4907